MW01247171

Shut Up and Eat!

The Unofficial Doctor Who Series Ate Cookbook

By:
Angela Pritchett

Artwork and Layout:
Ginger Hoesly

Additional Artwork:
Kara Dennison

Photos by Anita Bruckert

Table of Contents

Introduction

Doctor Who, that amazing show from the BBC that has been on television for over 50 years! I love it, I also love cooking! So after watching the first episode of Series 8, I decided to do a cookbook and show my love of Doctor Who and food! I mean come on, part of Deep Breath takes place in a restaurant (well a fake one at least.) So why not make a fun cook book that adults and children together can like? Exactly, why not! So I recruited my fantastic friend Kara, who I asked to do one bit of fantastic artwork for me, and she introduced me to Ginger and the rest of that is history (very wobbly history!)

I have been writing for years, and cooking ever since I can remember, but writing a cookbook? I had never done that before! And it was challenging! Making sure the recipes will taste good, making sure there is something for everyone, it was a huge challenge, but I feel all the time and effort was worth it and I am truly excited and so proud of this book! The food is good, the artwork is amazing, and hopefully it will all bring a smile to your face as you look through it!

The one thing I want you, the reader (and cook!) to take away from this book, is to have fun with it, enjoy the cooking process and enjoy the recipes while watching your favorite episode of Doctor Who!

So please, enjoy the recipes in this book, if you make them, please take photos (or even photos of you with the book!) I would love to see how people are using the book!

Episode 1:
Deep Breath

S.S. Marie Antoinette Broccoli Soup

Ingredients:
- 3 cups vegetable stock
- 2 cups chopped broccoli florets, can use fresh or frozen
- 1 small white onion, diced
- 1, 15 oz. can of evaporated milk
- 2 cups shredded cheddar cheese
- Salt and pepper to taste

Directions:
The S.S. Marie Antoinette is out of fuel, how else can you refuel than without a delicious warm soup to keep you going on those cold days at space, or sitting in London?

1. In a sauce pan mix vegetable stock, onions, and broccoli on high heat until the mixture begins to boil.
2. Reduce heat to medium, and check the onions, when they become tender add evaporated milk, and stir. Wait until mixture starts to simmer.
3. Remove from burner and mix in cheese until it is fully melted. Season with salt and pepper.

Spare Parts Beef Wellington

Ingredients:
- 1 onion
- 1 carrot
- 1 potato
- 1 celery stalk
- 1 cloves of garlic
- Olive oil
- 4 sprigs of Thyme
- ½ a cup of frozen peas
- 1 egg
- 1 pound of ground beef
- 1 package of puff pastry
- Flour for dusting
- Salt and pepper

Directions:

Need something to fill you up? Or to repair those "spare parts" that you got from that last body that came into the restaurant? The look no further than this easy beef wellington recipe.

1. Preheat oven to 350° F.
2. Remove pastry puff so it can get to room temperature.
3. Peel potato, dice potato, onion, and carrots; put mixture into a frying pan.
4. Put frying pan on medium heat and add 2 Tbsp. of olive oil.
5. Chop up your Thyme and garlic and add them.
6. Sauté everything until the vegetables are tender and onions are translucent.
7. Transfer mixture to a bowl to cool.
8. In a smaller bowl beat your egg.
9. Once vegetables are cooled add beef and peas, mix everything together and add salt and pepper, add half your egg into the mixture.
10. On a clean surface roll out your puff pastry.
11. Shape your beef mixture into a log in the center of the pastry. Brush the edges with some of the extra egg, roll up the rest of the pastry and tuck the edges in, brush with the egg.
12. Bake on a sheet in the preheated oven for 45 minutes to an hour until the pastry is a golden brown!

Out of This Time Roasted Potatoes

Ingredients:
- 1 Tbsp. olive oil
- 3 ½ lbs. Yukon Gold Potatoes
- 2 cloves garlic, minced
- ¼ cup Parmigiano-Reggiano, freshly grated
- Coarse salt
- Fresh ground pepper
- Fresh parsley

Directions:
A T-rex wasn't the only thing that tagged along with the Doctor into Victorian London! These delicious potatoes also came along!

1. Scrub and wash potatoes, and peel, place in a large pot, cover with water that is about two inches above the potatoes. Bring water to a boil and cook for 10-15 minutes until potatoes are tender.
2. Once potatoes are fork tender drain the water in the pot, allow to cool.
3. Preheat oven to 425° F.
4. Once potatoes have cool enough to touch cut them in half and cut the halves into quarters. Place potatoes cut sides down and cover with pepper and salt. Cook for 30-40 minutes. Halfway through rotate the potatoes.
5. Reduce oven heat to 350, turn potatoes over and sprinkle with garlic and Parmigiano-Reggiano as well as some more pepper and salt (if you like). Cook for 10-15 more minutes.
6. Remove from oven, sprinkle with parsley. Makes a great side for your Spare Parts Beef Wellington!

T-Rex Tooth Ache Blue Box Cookies

Ingredients:
- 2 ¾ cup flour
- 1 tsp baking soda
- ½ tsp. baking powder
- ½ tsp. salt
- 1 cup unsalted butter, at room temperature
- 1 ½ cup sugar
- 1 egg
- 1 tsp. mint extract
- 15-ish drops blue food coloring
- 1 bag of chocolate mints chips

Directions:

These delicious blue mint cookies will appease any T-Rex who may just happen to stumble along, but be care, too many can give you a tummy ache!

1. Preheat oven 375° F.
2. Sift the dry ingredients (flour, baking soda, baking powder and salt) together and set aside.
3. In a large bowl, cream together the butter and sugar until smooth. Beat in egg and mint extract. Gradually blend in the dry ingredients. Add blue food coloring, then add the chocolate mint chips.
4. Using a spoon, spoon small circles of the dough onto a wax paper lined cookie sheet.
5. Bake for 8-10 minutes, checking them so they do not burn.

Madam Vastra's Evening Punch

Ingredients:
- 1 - 2 liter Lemon Lime Soda
- 1 can, 46 oz. of Pineapple juice chilled
- 2 qt. bottle of white grape peach juice
- Bottle of Vodka (optional if you want Non-Alcoholic)
- Peaches, cut into slices

Directions:
After a long day of work Jenny likes to make this drink for Madam Vastra!

1. Take an ice cube tray and pour some of the pineapple juice into the tray, freeze for a few hours before making your drink.
2. In a large pitcher or punch bowl mix the entire bottle of lemon lime soda, white grape peach juice and pineapple juice together, stir. Add peach slices once mixture is done. You can also add equal parts of each to a cup, if you do not want to make an entire batch.

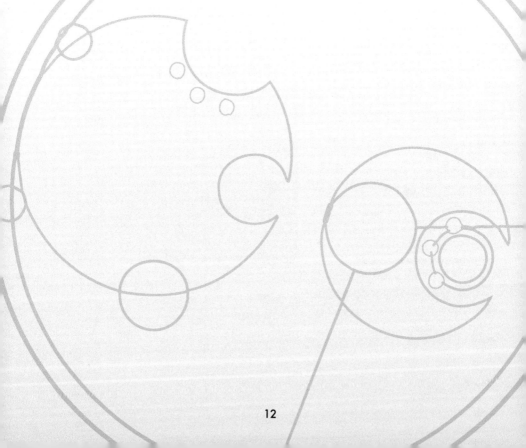

Episode 2:
Into the Dalek

Dalek Stuffed Peppers

Ingredients:
- 6 medium sized green peppers or 4 large Green peppers
- 1 ½ lbs. ground beef
- 1 onion
- 1 small can black olives
- ½ tsp. salt
- 2 cups shredded cheese of your choice
- 2 cups chopped tomatoes
- 1 ½ cups cooked rice

Directions:
Those pesky Daleks are everywhere! Show them you aren't going to give in and exterminate these peppers!

1. Cut off the tops of the peppers and remove the seeds. In a pot with a lid, boil water and add the peppers for 6 minutes with the top on. Remove when tender but crisp.
2. Brown beef and onions and salt in a skillet, drain, add the tomatoes and cheese and rice.
3. Fill each pepper with the filling and place in an oven safe dish, uncovered. Bake in the oven at 350° F for 20 minutes.
4. Cut the olives into halves. Remove the peppers, and add the Dalek bumps to the to of the peppers, and enjoy!

"Don't Be Lasagna" Rolls

ngredients:
- 9 lasagna noodles, cooked
- 1 (10 ounce) package frozen chopped spinach, thawed and drained
- 1 (15 ounce) container ricotta cheese
- 1/2 cup grated Parmesan cheese
- 1 egg
- ½ tsp. minced garlic
- ½ tsp. dried Italian seasonings
- Salt and pepper
- (optional) 1 chicken breast, cooked and diced
- 32 oz. tomato spaghetti sauce
- 9 Tbsp. mozzarella cheese, shredded

Directions:
1. Preheat the oven to 350° F. Drain the spinach, and mix with the ricotta, Parmesan cheese, egg, garlic, Italian seasonings, chicken (optional if you want it vegetarian), and salt and pepper in a mixing bowl.
2. Place a piece of wax paper on the counter and lay out each lasagna noodle, patting them dry if you need too. Spread the cheese and spinach mixture evenly onto each noodle. Gently roll each up and place each seam side down into a baking dish.
3. Use a spoon to pour the spaghetti sauce over each roll (use a lot or a little depending on how much sauce you like.) Then put the mozzarella over each one, cover baking dish with aluminum foil and bake for 35-40 minutes, until cheese has melted.

TARDIS Meringues Cookies

Ingredients:
- 3 egg whites
- 3 ½ Tbsp. blue raspberry gelatin desert mix
- Dash of salt
- 1 cup sugar
- 1 tsp. vinegar
- 6 oz. white chocolate chips

Directions:
Something is wrong with the chameleon circuit and the TARDS looks like meringue cookies!

1. Beat egg whites gradually adding gelatin mix and sugar until they are stiff and glossy.
2. Fold in vinegar and salt; beat well.
3. Add white chocolate chips.
4. Scoop a little onto a spoon and drop onto a greased cooking sheet.
5. Bake in the oven at 250° F for 40-50 minutes, checking on them occasionally to make sure they do not burn.

The Good Dalek

Ingredients:
- 3 ½ -4 tsp instant coffee (depending on how strong you like it)
  2 Tbsp. hot water
  ¼ cup caramel ice cream topping
- ½ cup milk
- ½ cup cold water
  Ice cubes

Directions:
You too can be a good Dalek!

1. In a glass mix the instant coffee and hot water until mixed.
2. Add the caramel ice cream topping and mix well.
3. Then add the milk and water and stir until combined.
4. Add ice and drink immediately.

17

Episode 3:
Robot of Sherwood

Sherwood Vegetable Lentil Stew

ngredients:
- 2 Tbsp. olive oil
- 2 cloves garlic
- 1 medium onion
- ½ lb. (3-4) carrots
- 3 celery sticks
- 1 (15 oz.) can black beans
- 1 cup brown lentils
- 1 tsp. cumin
- 1 tsp. oregano
- ½ tsp. smoked paprika
- ¼ tsp. cayenne pepper
- Freshly ground black pepper
- 1 (15 oz.) can petite diced tomatoes
- 4 cups vegetable broth
- ½ tsp. salt

Directions:
1. Mince the garlic and dice the onion. Cook both in a large pot with olive oil over medium heat until tender. Meanwhile, slice the celery and peel and slice the carrots. Add the celery and carrots to the pot and continue to sauté for about 5 more minutes.
2. Drain the can of black beans and add it to the pot along with the dry lentils, cumin, oregano, smoked paprika, cayenne pepper, and some freshly cracked pepper. Finally, add the diced tomatoes, their juices and vegetable broth, and stir to combine.
3. Increase the heat to medium high and allow the pot to come up to a boil. Once it reaches a boil, turn the heat down to low, place a lid on top, and let it simmer for 30 minutes. After 30 minutes, test the lentils to make sure they are tender. If not, continue to simmer until they are tender.
4. Taste the soup and add salt as needed. Serve hot.

Bullseye Steak Kabobs

Ingredients:
- 2 cups golden potatoes
- 2 lbs. sirloin (cut into cubes)
- 1 zucchini sliced thickly
- 1 onion sliced to fit on a skewer
- 1 Tbsp. fresh thyme
- 1 Tbsp. fresh rosemary
- ½ cup balsamic vinegar
- ½ cup olive oil
- 2 tsp. steak seasoning
- 3 garlic cloves (crushed)
- Wooden skewers

Directions:
1. Combine the thyme, rosemary, balsamic vinegar, olive oil, steak seasoning and garlic. In a bowl. Separate ½ of the mix into a small bowl.
2. Put steak in a bowl; pour the ½ of the marinade over steak and cover, set in fridge for 30 minutes.
3. Boil potatoes for 15 minutes until just under fork tender, drain.
4. Cut your zucchini and onions large enough to go on the skewers.
5. Pour the remaining half of the marinade over the onions and zucchini.
6. On wooden skewers put your steak, zucchini, onions and potatoes.
7. Place your skewers on the grill for 6-8 minutes (depending on how well you want them) turning them over throughout the process.

Robotic Cinnamon Baked Pears

Ingredients:
- 3 pears
- 3 tsp. cinnamon
- 2 tsp. sugar

Directions:
1. Preheat oven to 400° F.
2. Cut pears in half and core. Place in an oven dish and bake for 35 minutes. Pears should be slightly browned when done. Mix sugar and cinnamon together adjusting amounts of each to suit your taste.
3. Sprinkle with sugar and cinnamon mixture to taste and serve.

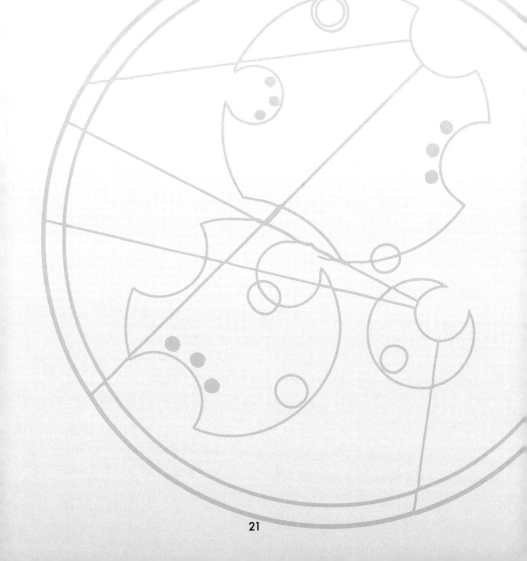

Merry Men's Raspberry Water

Ingredients:
- 7 or so raspberries
- Sparkling water
- Ice

Directions:
1. Fill your cup up about halfway with raspberries. With a spoon, crush the raspberries.
2. Pour your sparkling water into the cup over the crushed raspberries.
3. Add ice and enjoy this merry drink for all!

The Maiden Clara's Blood Orange Bellini

Ingredients:
- 5 Blood Oranges
- 1 bottle Prosecco

Directions:
1. Squeeze the juice from the blood oranges into a cup.
2. Mix equal parts blood orange juice and Prosecco into your chalice and enjoy!

Episode 4:
Listen

Little Time Lord Stuffed Turkey and Rice Peppers Soldiers

Ingredients:
- 4-5 small/medium bell peppers, Red, Orange and Yellow
- ⅓ cup uncooked rice (for medium peppers- adjust if needed)
- ¾ cup chopped onion
- 2 garlic cloves, about a Tbsp. or so minced
- ¾ cup diced tomatoes, w/juice (unsalted/unseasoned)
- ½ lb. ground turkey (or other meat you like)
- ¼ tsp. dried basil
- ¼ tsp. oregano
- ½ tsp. salt
- ½ tsp. pepper
- Pinch of allspice
- 1 Tbsp. chopped fresh basil
- ½ cup grated pepper jack cheese
- Fresh basil leaves, for garnish

Directions:
1. Finely chop onions
2. Add onion, garlic, and tomato together in a mixing bowl (tomatoes with their juice - it keeps the stuffing moist during cooking).
3. Add seasoning.
4. Chop basil and add to bowl and mix all ingredients.
5. Add raw meat and uncooked rice and mix.
6. Grate your cheese and set to the side.
7. Cut a hole in the top of the peppers and pull out the insides, remove remaining seed and rinse with cold water if needed.
8. Using a spoon, fill the peppers with the turkey mixture until it is just under the top (they will expand when cooking because of the rice).
9. Put all three peppers in the crock pot and add just a little water to the bottom of the crockpot so they will not stick to the bottom.
10. Put your cheese on the top of the peppers, cover the crock pot and cook on high for 5 hours (for softer peppers) or low for 6-7 hours (for peppers with a little crunch).
11. Once done cooking carefully remove the peppers from the crock pot and sprinkle a little more cheese on top and your little Time Lords are ready to eat!

'he Clara Under Your Bed Beef Stew

ngredients:
- 2 tsp. extra-virgin olive oil
- 4 slices turkey bacon, coarsely chopped
- 1 ½ cups finely chopped onion, (2 medium)
- 1 ½ cups diced carrots, (2 medium)
- ½ cup diced celery (1 stalk)
- 3 cups reduced-sodium beef broth
- 2 cups dry red wine, such as Merlot or Zinfandel
- 1 tsp. fresh thyme leaves, or 1/2 tsp. dried
- 2 bay leaves
- 2 2 ½-inch-long strips orange zest
- 3 ½-3 ¾ pounds Cubed Stewing Beef
- Freshly ground pepper, to taste
- ½ cup chopped watercress, or parsley

Directions:
1. Heat oil in a 4 to 5 quart Dutch oven over medium-high heat. Add bacon and cook, stirring often, until lightly browned, 3 to 5 minutes. Add onions, carrots and celery; cook, stirring often, until the vegetables are softened and lightly browned, 8 to 10 minutes. Add broth, wine, thyme, bay leaves and orange zest. Bring to a boil.
2. Place the beef in a 5 to 6 quart slow cooker and turn heat to high. Carefully pour the hot vegetable mixture over the beef. Put the lid on and cook until the beef is falling-apart tender when prodded with a fork, 6 to 7 hours.
3. To serve, ladle the stew into bowls and sprinkle with parsley.

The Young Doctor's Pillows

Ingredients:
- Frozen puff pastry sheets
- 1 cup mini marshmallows
- 1 cup hazelnut spread
- 1 egg white

Directions:
1. On a flat surface lay out your pastry sheets, cut into four equal squares.
2. Spread your hazelnut spread in the center of each square, leaving about half an inch for the edges, and add some mini marshmallows on top.
3. Fold over the pastry square and take a fork and crimple the edges of the folded square firmly.
4. Now make your egg white wash, take your egg white and mix it with one tablespoon water, brush wash over each puff.
5. Preheat your oven to 350° F, Bake for 23-25 minutes, let cool for 5 and then enjoy!

Dan the Soldier Man's
Caramel Stay Awake Drink

Ingredients:
- 10 oz. strong coffee
- ⅓ cup milk
- ⅓ cup caramel coffee creamer
- Whipped cream for topping
- Caramel drizzle for topping
- Powdered cinnamon

Directions:
Not sure about that monster under your bed? Trying to stay awake because you are scared something will get you in your sleep? Well Dan the Soldier Man is here for you, to help keep you wired and awake!

1. Brew 10 oz. of strong coffee, let cool and place in ice cube trays. Freeze.
2. Remove ice cubes, place in a blender, and add your caramel creamer, and milk, blend until smooth. Top with whipped cream and caramel drizzle and cinnamon.

Episode 5:
Time Heist

Ms. Delphox's Jalapeno Poppers

Ingredients:
- 12 jalapenos, halved and seeds removed
- 1 box puff pastry
- 1 cup cheddar, shredded
- 1 egg
- Olive oil
- 8 oz. cream cheese
- 4 cloves garlic

Directions:
All these Jalapeno poppers look the same! Much like all the Ms. Delphox clones, except these Jalapeno poppers are delicious and not as brutally bossy as Ms. Delphox (just don't tell her we said that.)

1. Set your oven to 400°F. Set out garlic cloves on a sheet of aluminum foil and drizzle the olive oil over them. Cover and roast for about 30 minutes.
2. Roll out pastry sheets and cut into 3x3 squares.
3. In a large bowl mix cream cheese, cheddar and garlic.
4. Spoon the cheese mixture onto each Jalapeno half.
5. Wrap the 3x3 squares around the Jalapenos and set on a baking sheet.
6. Whisk eggs together in a bowl with 3 Tbsp. water. Brush over covered jalapenos.
7. Bake in oven at 400°F for 20 minutes.

The Architect's Chicken Fettuccine

Ingredients:
- 8 oz. Fettuccine, cooked
- 3 Tbsp. extra virgin olive oil
- 3 boneless chicken breast, cubed
- Salt and pepper, to taste
- 1 pint grape tomatoes, halved
- ½ cup green olives, cut in half
- ¼ cup fresh flat leaf parsley

For Sauce:
- 2 Tbsp. extra virgin olive oil
- 1 lemon, juiced
- ⅛ tsp. garlic powder
- Salt and pepper, to taste
- Grated parmesan cheese

Directions:
You may not remember saying you love this pasta, but you did allow your memory to be wiped, so just take the Architect's word and dig in!

1. Heat olive oil in a large skillet and add chicken.
2. Season with salt and pepper, and cook until chicken is browned on all sides.
3. Add your grape tomatoes, green olives, and parsley, and stir. Continue cooking (and stirring) until chicken is completely cooked.
4. Add pasta to the skillet and cook until pasta is heated.
5. In a cup combine, lemon juice, olive oil, garlic powder, salt and pepper and stir until completely mixed together.
6. Stir sauce into pasta.
7. Season with salt and pepper to your liking, top with parmesan cheese.

The Teller's Key Lime Pie Dip

Ingredients:
- 1 cup key lime juice
- 2 cans condensed milk
- 2 packages cream cheese, room temperature
- Whipped topping (optional)

Directions:
Hopefully you don't have any guilty thoughts about this delicious dip, because The Teller will definitely be able to read your mind.

1. In a mixing bowl add the lime juice and condensed milk and cream cheese, stir until creamy and smooth.
2. Serve with gram crackers, and top it off with shipped topping if you like!

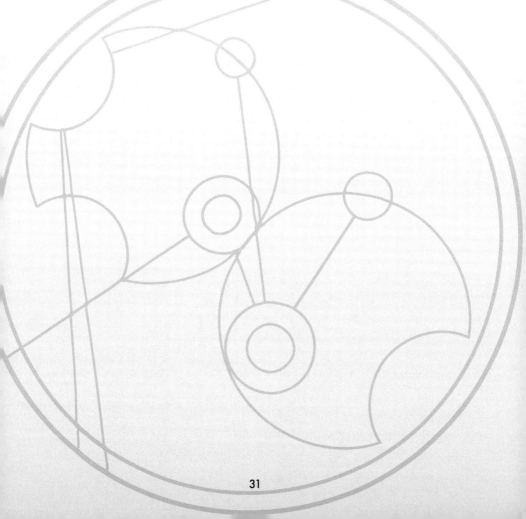

Karabraxos Cherry Cream Soda

Ingredients:
- Cherries (2 for each drink)
- Cream Soda
- Vodka
- Dark Cherry Juice

Directions:
Karabraxos isn't only known for its bank, but delicious cherry soda that Madam Karabraxos enjoys while she yells at her clones.

1. In a glass with ice cubes in it, fill half way with Dark Cherry Juice.
2. Add one shot of vodka.
3. Top it off with cream soda.
4. Add cherries to garnish.

Saibra's Shapeshifting Banana Raspberry Smoothie

Ingredients:
- ½ cup milk (could also use almond milk)
- 1 banana
- ½ cup raspberries
- 2 ice cubes
- 1 dollop hazelnut spread

Directions:
Just like Saibra, these ingredients shapeshift into a delicious smoothie that can be enjoyed during a bank heist, or just relaxing in your big blue time traveling ship!

1. Add ice, milk, raspberries, banana and hazelnut spread in your blender.
2. Blend until smooth, and pour in a cup.

Episode 6:
The Caretaker

Mr. Pink's Pasta Salad

Ingredients:
- 1 (16-ounce) box rotini tri-colored pasta, cooked
- 2 cans black beans rinsed and drained well
- 1 small bag frozen corn, thawed
- 2 tomatoes, diced
- 4 green onions, chopped
- ½ cup bell pepper, chopped
- ½ cup white onion, chopped
- 2-3 Tbsp. fresh cilantro chopped
- ¾ of a large bottle of zesty Italian dressing

Directions:
1. Prepare the pasta according to the box.
2. Mix all ingredients in a large bowl.
3. Cool in fridge and enjoy your delicious pasta salad worthy of a math teacher, definitely not a gym teacher!

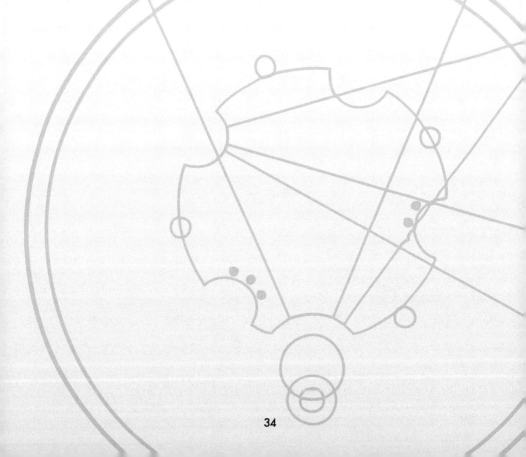

John Smith's Club Sandwich

Ingredients:
- 2 slices Texas toast or thick sliced bread
- 1 Tbsp. softened butter
- 2 tsp. mayonnaise
- 1 slice cheddar cheese
- 1 slice jack cheese
- 3 slices deli sliced ham
- 3 slices deli sliced turkey Breast
- 2 slices crispy thick Applewood bacon
- 2 thin slices tomato
- 2 tsp. honey barbecue sauce
- Lettuce

Directions:
1. Butter one side of each slice of bread and place butter sides down in skillet.
2. Cook until golden brown. Move to plate.
3. Stack ham slices, then turkey slices, then cheese slices in skillet over low until cheese melts.
4. Place one piece of bread toasted side down. Spread barbecue sauce on other side.
5. Transfer meat and cheeses from skillet on top of barbecue sauce. Add bacon slices on top. Top with tomato slices and shredded lettuce.
6. Take other slice of toast and spread mayonnaise on unbuttered side and place mayonnaise toward lettuce on top.
7. Slice diagonally and serve.

Coal Hill School
Peanut Butter Cookies

Ingredients:
- 1 cup peanut butter
- 1 cup sugar
- 1 egg
- A splash of vanilla extract

Directions:
A Coal Hill tradition!

1. Combine peanut butter, sugar, and egg well in a mixing bowl.
2. Drop tablespoon sized balls of dough on a cookie sheet. Smash down with a fork until more flat than round.
3. Bake at 350° for about 10 minutes. Be careful not to burn. Check on them to be safe!
4. They should be slightly brown on the bottom and soft.

Ms. Oswald's
Pineapple Mango Shake

Ingredients:
- 1 cup frozen mango
- ½ cup pineapple juice
- 6 oz. yogurt
- Sugar or sweetener to taste

Directions:
1. In a blender mix the ingredients and blend until smooth.

Episode 7:
Kill the Moon

Courtney's "Special" Moon Cheese Ball

Ingredients:
- 2 packs of 8 oz. plain cream cheese
- 1 packet of ranch mix
- 4 green onions sliced thinly
- 8 buttery crackers crumbled or Pita crisps crumbled

Directions:
1. In a bowl with a hand mixer, use the paddle attachment and beat the cream cheese until it is smooth. Add in the ranch mix and beat until well blended, then add the onions in.
2. Using a spatula, spoon the cream cheese mixture onto a large piece of plastic wrap. Wrap the cream cheese mixture into a ball shape with the plastic wrap. Remove the ball shape and roll over the crackers or pita crisps. Serve with veggies, crackers or pita crisps.

To the Galaxy and Beyond Chicken Corn Chowder

Ingredients:
- 3 pieces diced bacon
- 1 Tbsp. olive oil
- 4 boneless skinless chicken breasts
- 1 onion
- 3 celery stalks
- 2 carrots
- 3 minced garlic cloves
- 1 jalapeno pepper
- 2 cups milk
- 2 Tbsp. all-purpose flour
- ½ tsp. dried thyme
- 2 -20 oz. packages of frozen cream corn

Directions:
1. In a large soup pot with a lid, add bacon and olive oil. Chop carrots, celery, onions and garlic and add them to the pot (so many little planets in your galaxy to explore!) Stir frequently on medium heat until bacon is crisp (about 6 minutes.)
2. Remove the jalapeno stems, and insides (seeds, membrane, etc) and dice. Add to the pot.
3. Cut chicken breast into small pieces and add it to the pot. Add water to just cover all ingredients and put lid on. Cook for 20 minutes, until chicken is done.
4. Combine flour and milk in a small pan and cook, the mixture will become lightly brown, once it is add to the soup pot.
5. Add thawed packages of corn to pot. Sprinkle thyme into the pot, cover and cook for 20 more minutes on low heat.

Baby Moon Eggs

Ingredients:
- 8 oz. softened cream cheese
- 15 ½ oz. of vanilla creamed filled vanilla cookies (you can add one or two chocolate cookies if you want little babies hatching from the eggs)
- 8 oz. white melting chocolates

Directions:

The moon is an egg! And it is getting ready to hatch, so what would any companion do? Well it is time for desert! And these eggs are delicious! Get ready for some delicious cream cheese eggs, since you know, the moon isn't made from cheese, it is cream cheese.

1. Prepare oven tray with wax paper.
2. Blend the vanilla cookies in the blender or food processor until they are crumbled.
3. Pour crumbs in a bowl and mix in the softened cream cheese.
4. Mold the mixture into small balls and place on the oven tray.
5. Put oven tray in the freezer for an hour.
6. Melt the white chocolate in the microwave, at 5-10 second intervals until fully melted.
7. Using a fork dip each ball into the white chocolate and put them back on the oven tray.
8. Stick them into the fridge until the chocolate is cold, and enjoy! Store the remainder inthe fridge.

Hot Chocolate with Mini Moon Eggs

Ingredients:
- 4 cups milk
- 2/3 cup chocolate syrup
- 3 Tbsp. hot fudge topping
- Pinch of salt
- Tiny marshmallows

Directions:

Congrats! You have just saved the earth! Now it is time for some delicious hot chocolate with mini moon eggs!

1. Cook milk in a large nonaluminum sauce pan over medium heat, stirring frequently until thoroughly heated (about 6-8 minutes.) Do not let it boil.
2. Whisk in the chocolate syrup, fudge topping and salt, whisking vigorously until the chocolate is well blended and frothy.
3. Pour in your favorite Doctor Who mug, add some mini Moon eggs (marshmallows) and enjoy!

Episode 8:
Mummy on the Orient Express

Orient Express Spring Roles

Ingredients:
- 6 rice paper wrapper sheets (aka bahn trang in the Asian food store)
- A large bowl of water to dip rice paper sheets
- 1 small ripe mango, peeled and cut into strips (can also use cabbage or bean sprouts)
- 1 carrot, peeled and cut into match sticks
- 6 sprigs mint
- 6 sprigs cilantro
- 2 oz. dried rice sticks or rice vermicelli

Directions:
Ready for a delicious appetizer that may or may not resemble the mummy that is stalking the Orient Express? The check out these delicious goodies!

1. Soak the dried rice sticks in boiling water for 3 minutes and drain well.
2. Dip the rice paper sheets in water, making sure all sides are wet. Shake off excess water. Place on a clean work surface. Place a sprig each of cilantro and mint in the front 1/3rds of the rice paper sheet. Then place lettuce leaf, a little rice noodles, carrot, and mango slices.
3. Fold and roll the spring rolls. Fold the top of the circle, then the sides then roll onto the remaining side tightly and you have your spring roll to enjoy on your train ride across the universe!

First Class Chili Dipping Sauce

Ingredients:
- 4 Tbsp. rice vinegar
- 4 Tbsp. soy sauce
- 2 Tbsp. warm water
- 2 Tbsp. sugar
- Red pepper flakes
- 1 garlic clove peeled and crushed

Directions:
Whisk all the ingredients together, until sugar dissolves completely and enjoy with your Orient Express Spring Rolls!

Cruse of the Mummy Channa Wrap

Ingredients:
- 1 cup dried chickpeas, soaked overnight and boiled until tender
- 4- 8-inch tortillas wraps
- ¼ tsp. ground turmeric
- 1 tsp. salt
- 3 Tbsp. Madras-style curry powder
- 1 tsp. ground cumin
- ¼ tsp. cayenne
- 2 cups onions, diced
- 5 cloves garlic, minced
- ½ chili pepper, seeded and diced
- 1 (2x1-inch) hunk of fresh ginger, peeled and minced
- 2 Tbsp. olive oil
- Spinach

Directions:
Want something that's fun, wrapped up like a mummy, but won't kill you and delicious? Even the doctor would like these!

1. In a large skillet add olive oil. Heat, and cook onions until soft and translucent. Add garlic and chili pepper and garlic. Cook for three minutes, stirring constantly.
2. Add the curry powder, ground cumin, cayenne, turmeric, and salt. Stir well until it gets a paste-like consistency.
3. Add chick peas and about 3 cups water to the skillet. Bring to a simmer then lower heat, stirring regularly until most of the liquid has evaporated and there is a thick sauce.
4. Spoon out mixture on your tortilla wraps, add spinach and be prepared for a wrap to die for!

Perkin's Poached Pears

Ingredients:

4 pears, peeled
3.5 oz. icing/confectioner's sugar
Juice of ½ lemon
1 vanilla pod, open and scraped
4 cups water

Sauce:
• 3.5 oz. dark chocolate
• ⅓ cup heavy cream
Optional:
• Vanilla Ice Cream

Directions:

Every need a sweet pick me up after making sure that the orient express is running smoothly all day long? Then enjoy these delicious and sweet Poached Pears! Perkin's (and Gus) approved!

1. Put the 4 cups water into a saucepan, stir in the sugar, lemon juice and vanilla pod. Bring to a simmer and heat until the sugar has dissolved.
2. Carefully peel the pears, leave the stalks intact. Slice off a thin little disc at the base of each pear so that they can sit upright on a plate or bowl.
3. Place the pears into the hot syrup in the saucepan and cover with a piece of baking paper, make sure the pears are submerged in the syrup. Simmer the pears in the syrup for 20 minutes, then, using a small skewer, test them to see if they are tender. If not, cook for another 5 minutes and check again to see if tender. Once they are cooked, take the syrup off the burner and let the pears cool.
4. To make the chocolate sauce, put the chocolate and cream into a heatproof bowl set over a pan of simmering water (make sure the base of the bowl doesn't touch the water). Stir constantly as the chocolate melts until it has a smooth consistency. Be sure to watch this as chocolate will burn.
5. Drain the pears and place them on a plate or in a bowl. Pour the chocolate sauce over them, and if you wish, serve with a scoop of ice cream! Then sit down with your favorite train engineer and enjoy!

Mrs. Pitt's Long Life Concoction
(It will keep the Mummy's away...or not)

Ingredients:
- 1 liter ginger ale
- 12 oz. frozen limeade
- 10 oz. frozen strawberry daiquiri mix
- 2 cups rum

Directions:
Need to keep those pesky mummy's away that keep trying to drain your life force? Then look no further than Mrs. Pitt's long life concoction!

1. Thaw frozen mix and limeade.
2. In a cup, mix equal parts of ginger ale, run, frozen limeade and strawberry daiquiri mix. Enjoy! You can also use a large punch bowl and mix the ingredients for a larger amount if you are having a party on the Orient Express!

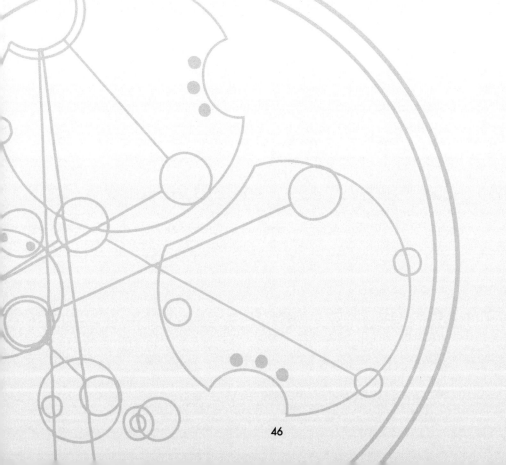

Episode 9:
Flatline

Blue Box Hummus and 2D Ships Pita Chips

Ingredients:
- 1 16 oz. can of chickpeas or garbanzo beans
- 1/4 cup liquid from can of chickpeas
- 3-5 Tbsp. lemon juice (depending on taste)
- 1 ½ Tbsp. tahini
- ½ to 1 clove of garlic, crushed (depending on taste)
- 1/2 tsp. salt
- 2 Tbsp. olive oil
- 1 seeded jalapeno pepper (optional if you don't like spice)
- 1-2 drops blue food coloring (optional if you do not want it blue in color)
- 4 pieces pita bread
- ¼ cup extra virgin olive oil
- Sea Salt and pepper for seasoning pita chips.

Directions:
This blue hummus and mini blue box pita chips are just what you need to help you figure out the perfect plan to fight these 2D boneless terrors!

1. Drain chickpeas and set aside liquid from can. Combine remaining ingredients in a food processor (or blender). Add ¼ cup of liquid from chickpeas. Blend for on low until thoroughly mixed and smooth. Add your 1-2 drops of blue food coloring last so you can decide on the color consistency you want.
2. Pour in a serving bowl; add olive oil and garnishes (I like to garnish with olives or parsley).
3. Brush the top of pita breads with olive oil and sprinkle with salt, ground black pepper.
4. Using a baby bottle shaped cookie cutter (you can find the metal ones at your local store, and they happen to look like a blue box we all love, you may have to bend it a little) cut out the shapes of your pita chips.
5. Place the pita slices on the oiled baking sheet. Let the pita chips bake at 400° F for about 10 minutes, depending on the thickness of pita bread, or until chips are golden brown and crisp. Be careful not the burn the chips.

2D Naan Pizzas

Ingredients: (makes two pizzas)
1 package of Naan Bread (two pieces)
1 Green Pepper, cut into squares
1 onion, cut into small pieces
Red pasta sauce
1 small can olives, cut into halves
1 sausage, boiled, cut into rounds
Shredded cheese

Directions:
Create your 2D piece of artwork on these pieces of Naan bread instead of the sides of walls in your city, easier to clean up and won't get you in trouble with the law!

1. On a baking sheet place your Naan bread.
2. With a spoon, spoon your red sauce over the naan bread.
3. Cover with shredded cheese
4. Add your sausage, green peppers, olives and onion.
5. Bake in the oven at 350° F for 10-15 minutes until cheese is melted.

Mini TARDIS Whoopie Pies

Ingredients:
- ½ cup butter, softened
- 1 cup sugar
- 1 egg
- 1 Tbsp. zest from one orange
- ½ tsp. salt
- 1 tsp. baking soda
- 1 cup milk
- 2½ cups flour
- Blue food coloring
- 1 container white vanilla icing

Directions:
These mini whoopee pies are just the size to fit inside the shrinking blue box so the doctor can have a snack while Clara figures out how to get him back to his normal size!

1. Preheat your oven to 375° F. In a bowl sift together the flour, baking soda and salt. In a mixer combine butter, shortening and brown sugar until combined into a cream. Add egg and orange zest and beat for 2 minutes. Turn your mixer on low and add half the flour and cocoa mix, add half the milk then repeat until the ingredients are all mixed together. Add blue food coloring until the color is even.
2. Line two baking sheets with parchment paper. Use a round spoon to drop mixture two inches apart from each other on the parchment paper.
3. Bake for 8-10 minutes until centers are set. Gently remove and cool on a silicone mat or towel. When cooled add your white cake icing.

Missy's Blackberry Sage Drink

Ingredients:
8 oz. of Blackberries
10 sage leaves
1 cup water
4 Tbsp. sugar
Club soda

Directions:
Missy is watching over everything that the Doctor and Clara are doing, so she needs something refreshing to drink while she conducts her plan!

1. In a small pot bring your 1 cup water to a boil and add in sugar, stir until it dissolves.
2. Crush sage leaves and add them to the water and sugar and let them sit for 15 minutes. Remove leaves after 15 minutes.
3. Puree your 8 oz. of Blackberries in a blender. Strain the mixture, then take a table spoon full of the puree and place it in a cup. Add a table spoon of the water/sugar/sage mixture, and then top it off with club soda.

Episode 10:
In the Forest of the Night

Night Forest Salad

Ingredients:
1 tsp Greek seasoning
½ cup dried cranberries
1 cup hot water
⅓ cup canola oil
1 Tbsp. light brown sugar
2 Tbsp. balsamic vinegar
1 Tbsp. rice wine vinegar
1 Tbsp. soy sauce
1 – 10 oz. package of mixed salad greens
2 large nectarines, peeled and cut
½ cup coarsely chopped walnuts
1 – 4oz. package of feta cheese

Directions:
1. Place cranberries in a small bowl, add 1 cup hot water and let sit for 5 minutes, then drain.
2. Whisk together the Greek seasoning, canola oil, light brown sugar, balsamic vinegar, rice wine vinegar and soy sauce in a large bowl.
3. Add cranberries, greens, nectarines, walnuts and feta, tossing gently.

London Forest
Potato Vegetable Gratin

Ingredients:
- ¾ cup vegetable or chicken broth
- 2 Tbsp. butter or margarine
- 1 ½ lbs. russet potatoes peeled and thinly sliced
- 1 lb. celery root trimmed, peeled, quartered and thinly sliced
- 1 lb. parsnips (about 6), peeled and thinly sliced
- 1 cup heavy cream (or whipping cream)
- 2 Tbsp. snipped fresh chives
- 1 ¼ tsp. salt
- ½ tsp. pepper
- 1 package shredded cheese

Directions:
1. Preheat your oven to 400° F in a shallow 3 ½-4 quart baking pan or casserole dish, combine vegetable or chicken broth and margarine. Place in oven while it preheats for about 5 minutes to melt margarine.
2. In a large bowl toss the potatoes, celery root and parsnips with 1 ¼ teaspoons salt and ½ teaspoon ground black pepper until mixed thoroughly. Add the bag of shredded cheese.
3. Remove baking pan from the oven and add broth mixture to vegetables, and stir, spoon vegetables into baking pan, cover with foil and bake for 40 minutes.
4. In a microwave safe cup heat the cream in the microwave for 40 seconds, pour over the baking mixture evenly and return to the oven for 35 minutes or until the top is golden brown and vegetables are tender. Let cool for 5-10 minutes and then serve.

Clara's Black Forest Cherry Cupcakes

Ingredients:
- 1 box chocolate cake mix
- 1 can cherry pie filling
- Whipped cream
- Cherries

Directions:
1. Prepare a cupcake pan with liners.
2. Follow instructions for preparing the chocolate cake mix as according to the box.
3. Before you pour into the cupcake pans, add the can of cherry pie filling to the mixture.
4. Bake the cupcakes according to the box recipe; use a tooth pick to check them to make sure they are completely done.
5. Take out of the oven and cool on a metal rack.
6. When cooled add the whip cream and a cherry to the top. Share with your favorite Time Lord!

Overnight at the Museum Cinnamon and Apple Granola Snac.

Ingredients:
- 2 cups rolled oats
- ½ cup uncooked (washed) quinoa
- 1 cup almonds
- ½ cup seeds (the Doctor likes a combination of sunflower & pumpkin seeds)
- ½ cup shredded coconut
- 2 tsp. ground cinnamon
- ½ tsp. ground nutmeg
- 1 large apple, diced
- ¼ - ½ cup unsweetened apple sauce
- 3 Tbsp. coconut oil
- 2-3 Tbsp. raw local honey
- 1 tsp. vanilla extract

Directions:
Spending the night in the museum with your teachers from school? Stuck in a tent all night with your mates? Well bring some of this yummy trail mix and you will be the most popular kid in class!

1. Preheat your oven to 320° F. Line a baking tray with baking paper.
2. Mix all dry ingredients (except apple, apple sauce, coconut oil, honey) in large mixing bowl.
3. Combine your apple, apple sauce, coconut oil and honey
4. Add the dry mixture to the wet mixture and mix the ingredients together until the dry ingredients are well coated.
5. Spread the mixture evenly on your baking tray, bake for 10 to 15 minutes, stir mixture so you do not get clumps or clusters and bake again for another 10 to 15 minutes until a golden brown. Check occasionally to avoid it all burning!
6. Take it out of the oven and let it all cool completely, store in an air tight plastic container or Mason jar.

Museum Field Trip Punch!

Ingredients:
- 1 – 2 ½ inch long cinnamon stick
- 5 whole cloves
- 5 thin ginger slices
- 2 – 16 oz. bottles of pomegranate juice
- 4 cups white grape juice
- ½ cup pineapple juice
- 1 – 2 liter bottle of ginger ale

Directions:
1. In a Dutch oven cook the cinnamon stick, cloves and ginger, over medium heat, stirring constantly for 3-5 minutes until the cinnamon is fragrant.
2. Gradually stir in the juices (except the ginger ale) bring to a boil over medium-high heat. Reduce the heat to medium-low once boiling and let simmer for 10 minutes.
3. Pour mixture through a strainer into a heat safe pitcher. Discard the solids, you can either serve hot this way or chill and add ginger ale for a more bubbly drink.
4. Great for those overnight museum field trips when you need to stay warm, or have a nice cool drink! Even Mr. Pink and Ms. Oswald would drink this with you!

Episode 11:
Dark Water

Time Paradox
Crab and Cream Cheese Wontons

Ingredients:
- 8 oz. crab
- 4 oz. cream cheese, at room temperature
- 2 cloves garlic, minced
- 2 green onions, thinly sliced
- 1 Tbsp. freshly grated ginger
- 1 tsp. sesame oil
- Salt and freshly ground black pepper, to taste
- 16 2-inch won ton wrappers
- 1 large egg, beaten

Directions:
1. Preheat oven to 400° F. Lightly oil a baking sheet or coat with nonstick spray.
2. In a large bowl, combine crab, cream cheese, garlic, green onions, ginger, sesame oil season with salt and pepper, to taste.
3. To assemble the wontons, place wrappers on a work surface. Spoon 1 ½ teaspoons of the mixture into the center of each wrapper.
4. Using your finger, rub the edges of the wrappers with egg. Fold all sides over the filling to create an "X", pinching the edges to seal.
5. Place wontons in a single layer onto the prepared baking sheet; coat with nonstick spray. Place into oven and bake for 10-12 minutes, or until golden brown and crisp, and enjoy a time paradox in your mouth!

Neathersphere Tilapia Parmesan

Ingredients:
- 4 Tilapia fillets
- ½ tsp. salt
- ½ tsp. pepper
- ½ tsp. garlic powder
- 1 Tbsp. olive oil
- 2 eggs
- ½ cup panko bread crumbs
- 1 cup marina sauce
- 1 package pasta
- ½ cup mozzarella cheese
- Grated parmesan cheese
- ¼ cup all-purpose flour

Directions:
1. In a shallow dish (like a pie plate) combine the bread crumbs, flour, Parmesan, salt, pepper, and garlic powder.
2. In a separate bowl beat 2 eggs, dip the fish fillets into the egg mixture and then into the bread crumb mixture.
3. Flip to coat both sides with the bread crumbs, pressing the fish down gently.
4. Remove and set on a plate, repeat with remaining fish.
5. Place all the fish into the skillet with olive at once.
6. Cook on each side for 3-5 min or until the crust is golden brown.
7. Spoon 2-3 Tbsp of marinara sauce on the top of the cooked fish and top with mozzarella and Parmesan cheese.
8. Remove from heat and cover with a lid to melt the cheese.
9. Serve over top of your favorite pasta and enjoy your final meal in the Nethersphere!

Danny Pink's Heart Earl Grey and Cherry Tarts

Ingredients:
- 3 oz. cherry juice
- 2 Tbsp. Earl Grey loose tea leaves
- 3 oz. granulated sugar
- 2 eggs
- 2 oz. unsalted butter, cut into pieces
- Cherries to garnish the tops
- Mini pie crusts

Directions:
1. To make the Earl Grey cherry curd, combine the cherry juice and tea leaves in a small saucepan. Heat to just a simmer and remove from heat. Let the tea leaves steep in the juice for 5 minutes. Pour the liquid through a fine-meshed sieve into a stainless steel bowl that fits atop your small saucepan, squeezing out as much as juice as you can. Wash your small saucepan clean and put just enough water so that when the bowl sits on the mouth of the pan, its bottom not touching the water.
2. Heat the water to simmer.
3. To the infused tea liquid in the bowl, add the sugar and eggs, whisking constantly. Cook until the mixture thickens to a soupy, thick, creamy texture.
4. Remove pan from heat and, piece by piece, whisk in the butter.
5. Once the emulsion has cooled, cover tightly and chill until ready to bake the tarts.
6. To assemble the tarts, take all your components out of the refrigerator. Place about 2 to 3 Tbsp of the Earl Grey Cherry curd per tart shell, or until almost to the rim.
7. Bake the tarts in the same 375° F oven, about 20 to 25 minutes, or until the curd sets a little bit, but is still jiggly underneath.
8. Let the baked tarts cool for 25 minutes, before topping with Cherries. Cut cherries in half and cover the tops of the tarts.

Dark Water

Ingredients:
- 1- 2 liter lemon lime soda
- 1- 2 quart bottle of blueberry juice
- 1- 2 quart bottle of pomegranate juice
- 1 bottle of vodka (optional)
- 1 bag of frozen blueberries
- 1 bag of frozen black berries

Directions:
1. In a pitcher pour equal parts of the lemon lime soda, blueberry juice and pomegranate juice, mix well.
2. If you want it alcoholic add equal parts of vodka and stir.
3. Add the frozen blue berries and blackberries (still frozen do not thaw, they will keep the drink chilled.) For fun throw in some glow ice cubes and you have your dark water!

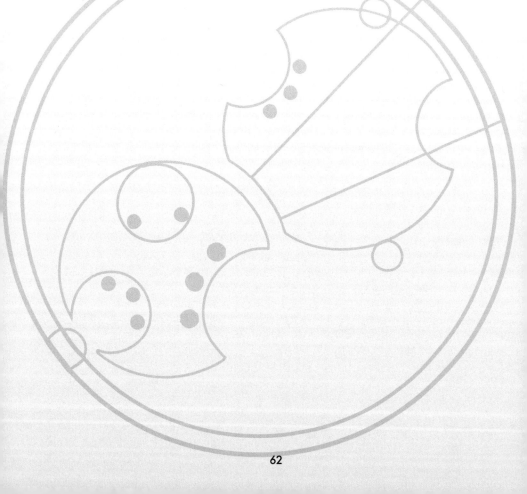

Episode 12:
Death in Heaven

Osgood's Favorite Zucchini Bites

Ingredients:
- ½ cup vegetable oil
- 1 cup Panko breadcrumbs
- ½ cup grated Parmesan cheese
- 2 zucchinis, thinly sliced into thick rounds
- ½ cup all-purpose flour
- 2 eggs, beaten

Directions:
1. Heat vegetable oil in a large skillet over medium high heat.
2. In a large bowl, combine Panko breadcrumbs and Parmesan; set aside.
3. Working in batches, cover zucchini rounds in flour, dip into eggs, then cover in Panko/Parmesan mixture, pressing to coat.
4. Add zucchini rounds to the skillet, 5 at a time, and cook until evenly golden and crispy, about 1 minute on each side.
5. Transfer to a paper towel-lined plate.

UNIT's Chicken Piccata

ngredients:
- 2 chicken breasts, pounded thin and butterflied
- Salt and pepper to taste
- 1 Tbsp. olive oil
- 1 Tbsp. butter
- 1 clove garlic, chopped
- ¼ cup dry white wine
- ½ cup chicken broth
- 1 lemon, juice
- 1 tsp. honey
- 2 Tbsp. capers
- 1 Tbsp. parsley, chopped
- One package pasta

Directions:
1. Heat the oil and 1 tablespoon of butter in a pan over medium heat.
2. Season the chicken with salt and pepper and fry until golden brown, about 2-3 minutes per side and set aside.
3. Add the garlic to the pan and sauté until fragrant, normally about a minute.
4. Add the wine to the pan and deglaze it.
5. Add the broth, lemon juice, honey and capers in the pan and simmer until the liquids have reduce by half, about 2-3 minutes.
6. Stir in the remaining tablespoon of butter, season with salt and pepper, mix in the parsley, return chicken to pan and toss to coat.
7. Prepare pasta according to the package and serve on the side of the chicken.

The Mistresses Decadent Chocolate Peanut Butter Bars

Ingredients:
- 2 cups white chocolate chips
- 1 cup peanut butter
- 2 cups chocolate chips
- 1 cup Reese's Peanut Butter Cup, chopped
- ½ cup heavy cream

Directions:
1. Line 8x8 inch pan with baking paper and set aside.
2. Melt white chocolate chips and stir in peanut butter and mix well until it's completely smooth.
3. Pour the mixture in the pan, tap it gently onto working surface to set and place in the freezer for 10-15 mins.
4. In a medium sauce pan over medium heat combine chocolate chips and heavy cream, stirring until the chocolate is completely melted and the mixture looks smooth.
5. Pour it over the hardened white chocolate layer and sprinkle with chopped peanut butter cups.
6. Set it in the refrigerator for a few hours, or if you are in a hurry place it in the freezer for half an hour.

The Grown Up Cyberman

Ingredients:
- 1 ½ shots of citrus vodka
  Splash of lavender simple syrup
- Double splash of home-made sweet n' sour
- Splash of Lemoncello
  Squeeze of fresh lemon wedge

Directions:
1. Add the ingredients in the specified proportions above in a glass stir and enjoy!

The Little Cyberman

Ingredients:
- 2 cups chocolate milk (can also use chocolate Almond Milk to make it nondairy)
- ¼ cup peanut butter
- 2 frozen bananas

Directions:
For all those little Cybermen out there that have just been converted, try this fun and delicious recipe!

1. In a blender mix your chocolate milk, peanut butter and bananas and blend until creamy. Pour into your favorite glass and enjoy!

Last Christmas

The Doctor's Mincemeat Pies

Ingredients for the Pastry:
- 5 oz. of plain flour
- 3 oz. of butter
- Pinch of salt
- Egg yolk

Ingredients for the Mince Pie:
- 2 apples, peeled, cored and sliced
- 8 oz. dried pears
- 8 oz. golden raisins
- 6 oz. dark brown sugar
- 2 oz. dried cherries
- 1 oz. crystallized gingers, chopped
- 2 oz. suet coarsely chopped
- 1 orange zested and juiced
- 1 lemon zested and juiced
- ¼ teaspoon grated allspice
- ½ cup brandy
- ½ teaspoon grated nutmeg
- ¼ teaspoon grated clove

Directions:
1. **Pastry**: rub together the 5 ounces of flour and 3 ounces of butter until it resembles fine crumbs.
2. Add the pinch of salt and egg yolk. If the mixture is too dry add a tablespoon of water, kneed the mixture together, wrap in plastic and put in the fridge to chill for an hour or so.
3. **Mince Meat:** Place all ingredients into a food processor and pulse to your thickness liking. Pour into a container and store in the fridge for two days.
4. Preheat the oven to 400°.
5. Take a cupcake or muffin tin out and spray it with nonstick cooking spray. Thinly roll out the pastry dough, cut into circles and gently place it into each cupcake/muffin slot. Fill each slot with a spoon full of the mincemeat filling. Cut a circle out of the dough and cover each slot gently pressing the edges to the bottle layer and the top together. Cut small steam holes in the top of each pie and cook for 20 minutes or until golden brown.

Clara's Turkey Wellington

Ingredients:
- 2 pound turkey breast
- 2 sheets frozen pastry puff, thawed
- 1 Tbsp. olive oil
- 2 Tbsp. butter
- 2 cloves minced garlic
- ¼ cup chopped onion
- 2 cups dry bread crumbs
- 4 Tbsp. turkey or chicken stock
- 1½ tbsp. dry chopped fresh thyme
- Salt and pepper to taste
- ½ cup frozen cranberries
- 1 egg
- 2 Tbsp. water

Directions:
1. Sauté the garlic and onions in the olive oil and butter for a few minutes.
2. Add the bread crumbs and toss until they begin to brown slightly.
3. Add thyme cranberries, salt and pepper. Add only enough stock so the stuffing holds together.
4. Line your cooking sheet with parchment paper; lay your pastry sheet on it.
5. Mix the 1 egg and 2 Tbsp. water together and make an egg wash.
6. Lay your turkey breast in the center of the pastry sheet. Brush the edges of the sheet with the egg wash.
7. Spoon the stuffing mix over top the turkey. Cover the top of the turkey and stuffing with the other pastry sheet. Press/pinch down on top of the bottom sheet and trim as need, press the pastry sheets together with your fingers.
8. Brush your egg wash over the entire top and sides of the top pastry sheet.
9. Bake at 400° F for 15-20 minutes; reduce the heat to 350° once the turkey has reached 170°. Continue cooking for 40-45 more minutes. Take out of the oven, let set for 10-15 minutes then cut and serve!

Twelve's Mocha Yule Log

Ingredients:
- 5 eggs, separated
  - ½ cup cake flour
- 1 cup sugar, divided
- ¼ tsp. salt
- ¼ cup baking cocoa
- ½ tsp. cream of tartar

Mocha Filling:
- 1½ tsp. instant coffee
- ⅓ cup butter, room temperature
- ½ cup confectioners' sugar

Mocha Frosting:
- ⅓ cup baking cocoa
- ⅓ cup butter room temperature
- 1½ tsp. vanilla extract
- 1 Tbsp. brewed coffee
- 2 cups confectioners' sugar
- 3 Tbsp. milk

Directions:
1. **Cake:** Set oven to 350° F. Line a 15X10 inch pan that is one inch deep with parchment paper. Grease the paper. Place egg whites aside and let them reach room temperature.
2. In a mixing bowl take the egg yolks, and beat until they are light and fluffy. Gradually add the ½ a cup of sugar to them, beat until mixture is thick. Combine the salt, cocoa and flour, and gradually mix into the eggs mixture until well blended.
3. Beat the egg whites until they are a foamy mixture and gradually add the cream of tartar, beat again, then add the other ½ cup sugar, a little at a time. Then add to the cocoa mixture, mix well until no streaks are in the mixture. Spread the mixture evenly into the pan and bake for 12-15 minutes. Let cake cool for 5 minutes them move to a linen towel dusted with confectioners' sugar, gently remove the parchment paper. Gently roll the cake up into the towel and let cool.
4. **Filling:** In a mixing bowl, beat the cream until it thickens, add sugar and coffee granules. Beat the mixture until peaks form. Chill the mixture. Gently unroll the cake, spread the filling and reroll the cake, place on a platter and chill.
5. **Icing:** In a mixing bowl beat frosting ingredients, apply frosting to the outside of the cake. With a fork add bark designs to the outside!

Santa's Tangerine Cream Tart

Ingredients:
- 3 egg yolks
- 1 tsp. finely grated clementine zest
- ¼ cup freshly squeezed clementine juice (about 2-3 clementines)
- 2 Tbsp. freshly squeezed lemon juice (about ½ a lemon)
- ¼ cup granulated sugar
- 3 Tbsp. cold unsalted butter, cut into small pieces
- Whipped topping
- 15 small pie shells

Directions:
1. Make the curd: Combine the egg yolks, clementine zest, clementine juice, lemon juice, and granulated sugar in a medium saucepan set over medium heat.
2. Cook, whisking constantly, until thickened, 5 to 7 minutes. Whisk in the butter. Remove the saucepan from heat and transfer the curd to a small bowl. Let cool completely. Refrigerate until ready to use.
3. Spoon tangerine curd into small pie shells, top with whipped topping!

Face Hugger Wassail

Ingredients:
- 2 quarts apple cider
- 2 cups orange juice
- ½ cup lemon juice
- 12 whole cloves
- 4 cinnamon sticks
- 1 pinch ground ginger
- 1 pinch ground nutmeg
- 1 ½ inch piece of fresh ginger, cut into slices
- 1 apple, sliced into rounds
- 1 orange, sliced into rounds

Directions:
1. In a crock pot, place all the ingredients in it, set on high and leave for 3-4 hours. The fruit should be soft and the color will have gotten darker.

Metric Conversion

Volume Conversions

U.S. Volume Measure	Metric Equivalent
1/8 teaspoon	0.5 milliliters
¼ teaspoon	1 milliliters
½ teaspoon	2 milliliters
1 teaspoon	5 milliliters
½ tablespoon	7 milliliters
1 tablespoon (3 teaspoons)	15 milliliters
2 tablespoon (1 fluid ounce)	30 milliliters
¼ cup (4 tablespoons)	60 milliliters
1/3 cup	90 milliliters
¼ (4 fluid ounces)	125 milliliters
2/3 cup	160 milliliters
¾ cup (6 fluid ounces)	180 milliliters
1 cup (16 tablespoons)	250 milliliters
1 pint (2 cups)	500 milliliters
1 quart (4 cups)	1 liter

Weight Conversions

U.S. Volume Measure	Metric Equivalent
½ ounce	15 grams
1 ounce	30 grams
2 ounce	60 grams
3 ounce	85 grams
¼ pound (4 ounces)	115 grams
½ pound (8 ounces)	225 grams
¾ pound (12 ounces)	340 grams
1 pound (16 ounces)	454 grams

Oven Temperatures

Degrees Fahrenheit	Degrees Celsius
200 degrees F	95 degrees C
250 degrees F	120 degrees C
275 degrees F	135 degrees C
300 degrees F	150 degrees C
325 degrees F	160 degrees C
350 degrees F	180 degrees C
375 degrees F	190 degrees C
400 degrees F	205 degrees C
427 degrees F	220 degrees C
450 degrees F	230 degrees C

Common Abbreviations

Abbreviation	Measurement
t or tsp.	Teaspoon
T or Tbsp.	Tablespoon
c.	Cup
Pt.	Pint
Qt.	Quart
Oz.	Ounce
lb.	Pound
Pkg.	Package

Recipe Notes

_____
_____
_____
_____
_____
_____
_____
_____
_____
_____
_____
_____
_____
_____
_____
_____
_____

Recipe Notes

Recipe Notes

_____

_____

_____

_____

_____

_____

_____

_____

_____

_____

_____

_____

_____

_____

_____

_____

_____

_____

Appendix

Appendix

Alcoholic Drinks:

Desserts:

About the Author and Artists

Angela Pritchett

Angela Pritchett is an American actress, writer, makeup artist and costumer originally from Virginia. She got her undergraduate and master degrees in Music Education, Liberal Studies and Ethnomusicology from the University of North Carolina at Greensboro. She worked as a Band and Orchestra teacher for almost ten years in North Carolina, while also acting and writing up a storm! Angela had many short stories and essays published in numerous anthologies that you can find at amazon.com/author/angelapritchett. When she is not working diligently on a project Angela is and avid cook, and foodie, she is also a co-host of "The Girls Who Waited; The Geek Girl YouTube show about Doctor Who and More!" She also loves chilling out with her cats and her Pug, Jimmy. You can find her online at: Twitter and Instagram: @Angalese, http://angelapritchett.blogspot.com/

Ginger Hoesly

Ginger is a graphic designer, illustrator, and would be a writer more often if she had the time. She received her BFA in illustration from Northern Illinois University (along with a minor in English) and currently spends her days in the print industry while drawing at every other waking moment. Her art can be seen on Instagram @randomthunk, while prints and other things can be purchased on Etsy and RedBubble at randomthunksarts. She engages in various shenanigans around the internet, but you'll have to find her for those. And if you're into this sort of thing, her portfolio is online at gingerhoesly.com (how convenient is that).

Kara Dennison

Kara is a writer, anime and video game editor, artist, cosplayer, and performer from Virginia. At present, she is the community manager and main blogger for (Re)Generation Who, the mid-Atlantic's new Doctor Who fan convention. Ask her anything about tea, guinea pigs, Arthurian legends, or Whovian minutiae. Visit karadennison.com for more.

Anita Bruckert

Anita is a multi-media artist who focuses on primitive emotions in her artwork. She has followed her love for art from the theater to the canvas and everywhere in between. She holds degrees in art, a Masters in Education, and enjoys her work as a licensed optician.

Thank You

So many amazing people helped make this book happen! Without the support of my amazing friends and family I would not have been able to get this done! First off Kara for being super supportive and introducing me to Ginger! You are an amazing friend, Kara, and I appreciate the support and confidence you gave me to get this book made (and thank you for doing artwork for it too! The piece still makes me giggle.) Ginger, you are a fantastic artist and I am so lucky to have your artwork in this book! Thank you so much for agreeing to do it, and for formatting the book! It looks better than I would have ever imagined! To Anita for making, trying and doing photos of the food! Your schedule is so crazy and busy and you still did what you could to help me! To Oni for giving me words of confidence when I was ready to throw this book out the door and not publish it, you are a good friend and an amazing person to support all the artists and people that you do. To my parents and grandma who support every crazy idea I have. And to everyone else who has supported me in this long endeavor to write a cookbook. Your support means more than any of you would ever know!

-Angela

I'd mostly like to thank the people who had to listen to me talk about this book for months, and what I was drawing, and for helping me brainstorm ideas that I typically ignored. Mostly I'm greteful for Kara hooking me up with Angela and this project as a whole, and to Angela for allowing me to draw things like "the Doctor kicking Robin Hood in the face". Thanks to my family for understanding I was anti-social because I was working on a book, to my boss for making me use Illustrator and understand it's actually pretty good for layouts, and to my tablet for not failing.

-Ginger

Made in the USA
Middletown, DE
24 December 2019